W9-DIR-891

WORLD HISTORY   1250–300 B.C.

Greek Civilization

PICTURE CREDITS
Cover, 3 top, 16–17, 50, 52–53, 57, 62 National Geographic Image Collection; pages 1, 6, 36, 47, 58 bottom, 60 Scala/Art Resource, NY; pages 3 middle, 14–15 H.M. Herget/National Geographic Image Collection; pages 3 middle, 14 British Museum, London, UK/Bridgeman Art Library; pages 3 bottom, 30 Attar Mehar/Corbis Sygma; pages 3 bottom, 57 Gian Berto Vanni/Corbis; pages 4–5 Roger Wood/Corbis; pages 8, 20, 26 James L. Stanfield/National Geographic Image Collection; pages 9 top, 13 bottom Reunion Musees des Nationaux/Art Resource, NY; pages 9 middle, 40 bottom akg-images, London; pages 9 bottom, 42–45 background Bettmann/Corbis; pages 10–11 Kevin Fleming/National Geographic Image Collection; pages 12–13 Stone/Getty Images; page 18 Alinari/Art Resource, NY; pages 20 bottom, 56 Archaeological Museum, Olympia, Archaia, Greece/Bridgeman Art Library; page 21 Kim Cheung/Reuters/Corbis; pages 22–23 Premium Stock/Corbis; pages 24, 42 right The Granger Collection; pages 27, 48, 53 Araldo de Luca/Corbis; page 28 left Museo della Civilita Romana, Rome/Bridgeman Art Library; pages 28 right, 51 Bildarchiv Preussischer Kulturbesitz/Art Resource, NY; page 29 top William H. Bond/National Geographic Image Collection; page 29 bottom Wadsworth Atheneum Museum of Art, Hartford, CT, Gift of Pierpont Morgan; pages 30, 36–37, 44, 59 Erich Lessing/Art Resource, NY; pages 30–31 background Delimont, Herbig, and Associates; pages 30–31 foreground R. Sheridan/Ancient Art and Architecture; page 31 Art Archive/Picture Desk; page 34 Nimatallah/Art Resource, NY; page 35 Art Resource, NY; pages 38–39 Robert C. Magis/ National Geographic Image Collection; page 40 left Todd A. Gipstein/Corbis; page 41 Kamal Kishon/Reuters/Corbis; page 42 Stock Montage; page 45 Christel Gerstenberg/Corbis; pages 46–47 AFP/Getty Images; page 49 William Cook/National Geographic Image Collection; page 54 HIP/Scala/Art Resource, NY; page 61 Ron Watts/Corbis.

Produced through the worldwide resources of the National Geographic Society, John M. Fahey, Jr., President and Chief Executive Officer; Gilbert M. Grosvenor, Chairman of the Board; Nina D. Hoffman, Executive Vice President and President, Books and Education Publishing Group.

PREPARED BY NATIONAL GEOGRAPHIC SCHOOL PUBLISHING
Ericka Markman, Senior Vice President and President Children's Books and Education Publishing Group; Steve Mico, Senior Vice President, Editorial Director; Marianne Hiland, Executive Editor; Richard Easby, Editorial Manager; Anita Schwartz, Project Editor; Jim Hiscott, Design Manager; Kristin Hanneman, Illustrations Manager; Matt Wascavage, Manager of Publishing Services; Sean Philpotts, Production Manager; Jane Ponton, Production Artist.

MANUFACTURING AND QUALITY MANAGEMENT
Christopher A. Liedel, Chief Financial Officer; Phillip L. Schlosser, Director; Clifton M. Brown III, Manager.

ART DIRECTION Dan Banks, Project Design Company

CONSULTANT/REVIEWER
Dr. Cynthia W. Shelmerdine, Robert M. Armstrong Centennial Professor of Classics, University of Texas at Austin

BOOK DEVELOPMENT Nieman Inc.

BOOK DESIGN Three Communication Design, LLC

PICTURE EDITING Paula McLeod, Worth a Thousand Words, Inc.

MAP DEVELOPMENT AND PRODUCTION Mapping Specialists, Ltd.

Published by the National Geographic Society
1145 17th Street, N.W.
Washington, D.C. 20036-4688

ISBN: 0-7922-4940-2

13 12 11 10 09
10 9 8 7 6 5 4 3

cover: Bronze sculpture of goddess Athena, patron of Athens **page 1:** Greek pitcher showing lions and other animals **page 3** (top): Olympic athletes running in full armor **page 3** (center left top): Reconstruction of Greek ships **page 3** (center right): Vase showing people harvesting olives **page 3** (center left bottom): The Acropolis in Athens **page 3** (bottom): Gold "Mask of Agamemnon" from Mycenae

4 INTRODUCTION

56 OVERVIEW

Greek Civilization

The civilization of ancient Greece first defined what *classical* means. A classical civilization values reason, learning, and the importance of the individual. Its art expresses simplicity, order, and ideal beauty. Many of the values and beliefs that define our society today can be traced back to ancient Greece.

The columns of this ruined Greek temple on the island of Sicily still display the simple beauty of classical architecture.

GREEK CIVILIZATION developed in a region of steep mountains and deep valleys, jagged coastlines and rocky islands. The rugged landscape of Greece encouraged the ancient Greeks to develop small, independent communities, or **city-states**. A city-state included a city and the villages of the surrounding countryside. Each city-state had its own local government. What united the Greeks as a people was not a single government, but a shared culture. They called this shared way of life *hellenikon*, or "Greekness."

At the beginning of Greek civilization is the tale of the Trojan War. The ancient Greeks believed that long ago their ancestors had sent a huge fleet to attack Troy, a city across the Aegean Sea in Ionia. Hundreds of years later, the great Greek poet Homer told the story of this expedition, called the Trojan War,

Ancient Greek statue of the type known as a *kore*, or maiden

Length of Recorded History

3000 B.C. Writing invented in Near East

1250 B.C.
The Trojan War

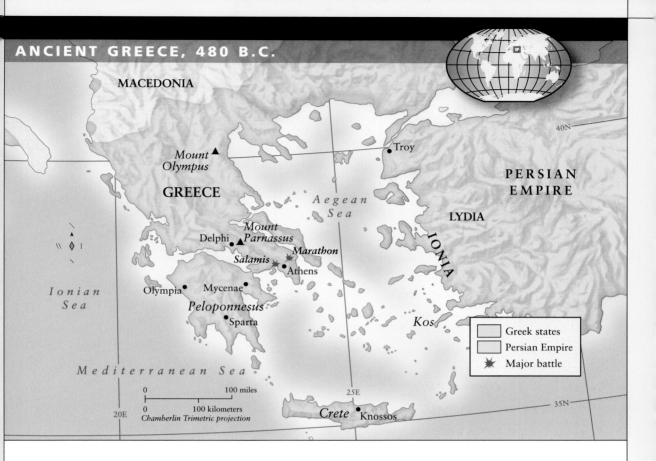

MACEDONIA

Mount Olympus ▲

GREECE

Aegean Sea

Troy

PERSIAN EMPIRE

LYDIA

Mount Parnassus ▲
Delphi
Salamis
Marathon
Athens

IONIA

Ionian Sea

Olympia
Mycenae
Peloponnesus
Sparta

Kos

Mediterranean Sea

	Greek states
	Persian Empire
✹	Major battle

0   100 miles
0   100 kilometers
Chamberlin Trimetric projection

20E   25E

Crete • Knossos

35N

40N

in his poems the *Iliad* and the *Odyssey*. All Greeks knew Homer's tales.

The ancient Greeks also shared a belief in a family of gods thought to live on Mount Olympus, the highest point in Greece. The Greeks worshiped these gods and went to their **sanctuaries,** or sacred shrines, to seek advice.

The most famous Greek sanctuary was Delphi, which was sacred to the god Apollo.

Athletic contests were also an important part of ancient Greek civilization. The **Olympic Games,** held every four years beginning in 776 B.C., were the greatest of these contests.

A.D. 1   A.D. 2000

After 300 B.C.
Greece in decline

Two Greek city-states, Athens and Sparta, created very different societies. The Athenians prided themselves on their ability to do many things well, from sailing a ship to building a temple. Spartans focused their efforts on always being ready for war.

Between about 480 and 430 B.C., ancient Greek civilization reached its height in Athens. This period is often called the Golden Age. By about 500 B.C., Athens had developed a **democracy** that became the forerunner of democratic government in the modern world. The ancient Greeks also developed new ways of explaining what happened in the world around them. They began to use observation and reason to help them understand the mysteries of life, instead of turning to the gods. This revolution in thinking is the beginning of science.

Athens and Sparta fought a long war for control of the Greek world, which left Greece very weak. Less than a century later, Alexander the Great of Macedon conquered the Greeks and spread Greek culture throughout his vast empire, which stretched from Egypt to India.

The articles in this book describe how civilization developed and flourished in ancient Greece and how Greek legends have continued to fascinate people ever since. To guide your reading, the articles have been organized around the following three **BIG IDEAS:**

1 Divided by geography, the ancient Greeks were united by a shared way of life.

2 Greek civilization produced enduring achievements in art, government, and science.

3 Greek legends have fascinated people ever since ancient times.

As you read, keep these ideas in mind. They will help you understand the most important characteristics and achievements of Greek civilization.

BIG IDEA: A SHARED CULTURE

Their worship of the Olympian gods was something that all Greeks shared.

BIG IDEA: LEGACY OF ANCIENT GREECE

For the Greeks of Athens, drama was a way to confront current political and cultural problems.

BIG IDEA: THE POWER OF LEGEND

Greek stories, such as those of the Trojan War, inspired later writers and artists.

Down to the Sea in Ships

An ancient Greek historian said that the Greeks were connected by "shared blood, shared language, shared religion, and shared customs." He was right about these links, but he left out one vital part of Greekness—the sea.

Ancient Greek sailors prayed to Poseidon, god of the sea, to grant them a safe voyage.

"We Greeks live around the sea like frogs around a pond."

— Plato, Greek thinker

Put yourself in the place of one of the gods of ancient Greek myths. You stand atop Mount Olympus. Greece is wild and rugged, with rocky cliffs, steep hillsides, and small villages. There is very little flat land for farming and few roads of any size. Beyond the land lies the sea. The deep blue waters of the Mediterranean Sea surround almost all of Greece. The water frequently cuts deeply into the land, making the coastline sharp and jagged. In a country like this, farming is difficult, so the ancient Greeks turned to the sea.

Catch of the Day

From your vantage point on Mount Olympus, you take a closer look at a stretch of coastline. Greek fishermen have just brought two small boats to the shore. Each boat is full of freshly caught fish. One man sits nearby on the rocky beach, patching holes in his fishing nets. In ancient Greece, fishermen mainly used nets, but they also fished with hooks and lines. Other fishermen unload the boats and pack the fish into baskets. They have caught herring and octopus

Harbor at Mykonos, one of
the Greek islands

Fish Sauce, Anyone?

The ancient Greeks were fond of a salty fish sauce. They poured it on everything, the way Americans use catsup. Here is one recipe.

First, you need a big jar and some fatty fish, such as sardines. At the bottom of the jar, put a layer of dried herbs with strong flavors, such as dill, coriander, fennel, celery, mint, and oregano.

Then, put down a layer of fish. If the fish are small, leave them whole; if large, cut them in pieces. Over this, add a layer of salt two fingers high.

Repeat these layers until the jar is filled. Let it rest in the sun for seven days. Then, mix the sauce daily for 20 days until it becomes a liquid.

and some of the larger fish that the Greeks called *thunnos* (from which our word *tuna* comes).

More boats approach the shore. Oars flash in the sunlight as they dip in and out of the water. These Greek men know the sea—and how to handle a boat. Each day, Greek fishermen head out into the Mediterranean to catch fish for their families and to sell at nearby marketplaces. You breathe in, enjoying the salty tang of the sea and the smell of fresh fish. No doubt about it, the ancient Greeks are a seafaring people, and fish is a major part of their diet.

Trade and Conquest

Ships were important to both trade and defense in ancient Greece.

Among the small fishing boats, you can see a larger merchant ship. Sailors are loading it with jars full of olive oil and wine. This merchant ship is bound northward to ports on the coast of the Black Sea. It will return carrying such goods as grain, metal, and timber, as well as human cargo, slaves. These people are prisoners of war who will be bought and sold at slave markets. The ship has an eye painted on each side of the prow, the front of the ship. Ancient Greek sailors believe that the painted eyes help guide their ships.

A Greek amphora shows men harvesting olives.

The voyage will be long, and there are always such risks as storms and pirates. However, to these Greek sailors, the sea is as much their home as the land.

Farther out, you can see part of a Greek city-state's navy, sailing westward. Its oars move in a steady rhythm, propelling the ship swiftly through the water. At the front is a ram in the shape of an animal's head. In battle, this ram will be driven into the sides of enemy ships. The ancient Greeks used their naval power to protect their **colonies,** areas that they controlled, located throughout the Mediterranean and Black Sea regions.

These colonies encouraged the growth of trade and industry in ancient Greece and helped spread Greek culture.

▶ *For more information about the geography of Greece, see page 56.*

WHY IT MATTERS TODAY

The geography of Greece has shaped Greek history and culture from ancient times to the present. By dividing the Greeks, geography encouraged the growth of independent Greek city-states. By linking the Greeks to the sea, geography helped develop and spread Greek civilization throughout the Mediterranean world.

Running in full armor was an Olympic sport.

GOING TO THE
GAMES

For the ancient Greeks, training the body was as important as training the mind. From very early in their history, the Greeks celebrated physical strength and competition in athletic games. The most famous Greek games were those held every four years at Olympia.

The entire ancient Greek world seems to be on the move on this hot August day. All roads leading to Olympia are jammed. Thousands of people are heading toward the Olympic Games. The games are held every four years to honor the god Zeus (zoos).

All free Greek men are eligible to participate in the games, but only the best of the best make it to Olympia. The athletes have been training for at least ten months to build up their strength for the difficult events.

A sacred truce is declared during the games to protect visitors. That means that soldiers from city-states who are at war with each other cannot attack people traveling to attend the games and worship at the great Temple of Zeus at Olympia.

Artists celebrated Olympic victors by creating statues like this one of a Greek discus thrower.

Everyone wants to witness the glory of Greece's best athletes! Citizens from Greek colonies as far away as Italy and the north coast of Africa make their way to Olympia, a plain in southern Greece. The mountain passes are filled with people traveling by foot and on horseback. Barges head up the river bringing government officials and nobles. Poets and artists are coming too. They will celebrate the victors in words and statues.

As they approach Olympia, the spectators gaze at the beautiful buildings. All will enter the Temple of Zeus to see its huge ivory and gold statue of the god that almost touches the ceiling. Important visitors and officials stay at the Guest House, while most spectators camp in tents and shelters—or just sleep on the ground—throughout Olympia.

Let The Games Begin!

The purple-robed judges lead a procession into Olympia on the first day of the festival. Judges and athletes take vows to uphold the fairness of the games. The next morning, thousands gather at the Hippodrome, an outdoor oval race course. They have come to watch the chariot and horse races.

Fans go wild during the contests, especially when two chariots smash into each other on the crowded track.

The spectators then move to the stadium to watch athletes compete in the **pentathlon.** This important competition consists of five separate events: a discus throw, a long jump, a javelin throw, a footrace, and a wrestling match. Every spectator has a good seat because the sides of the stadium slope. They can even refresh themselves from the heat at the water channel trackside.

On the third day, 100 bulls are sacrificed in a solemn ceremony at the altar to Zeus. The rest of the day is devoted to contests for young men between 17 and 20. The winners dream of the day when they will be able to compete in the men's events.

Crowds jam the stadium the next morning for the popular footraces. The slim, long-legged runners are later replaced by muscular wrestlers and boxers. The fans scream during the **pankration,** a savage combination of wrestling and boxing.

In the final event, soldiers called **hoplites,** wearing heavy armor, race the length of the stadium twice. This looks more like a military display than an athletic event, reminding the spectators that when the games end, so does the sacred truce.

Columns unearthed at Olympia

An Olympic medal that dates back to A.D. 3

The Thrill of Victory

It is the last day of the Olympic Games and time to honor the winners! At the Temple of Zeus, the judges place wreaths of olive branches on the athletes' heads. The spectators shower the winners with flowers. That night, the athletes attend a great banquet. Visitors to Olympia pack up their belongings and prepare for their long journey home.

The Olympic Games were held for about 1,000 years. When the Romans ruled Greece, a Roman emperor, who was a Christian, objected to the Greek worship of Zeus. He ordered the games ended in A.D. 393.

The site at Olympia slowly fell into ruin. The Temple of Zeus burned down, and wind, floods, and earthquakes covered the sacred site in mud. No trace remained of the magnificent buildings that once stood there. It was not until the late 1800s that **archaeologists,** scientists who study the remains of peoples and cultures of the past, rediscovered the site.

▶ *For more information about the Greek legacy, see page 62.*

WHY IT MATTERS TODAY

Today's Olympic Games are one of the best known legacies from ancient Greece. In today's Olympics, women are equally important participants. Today, the Olympics are global as well. To link to the past, the Olympic torch is lit in the ancient site at Olympia. The torch is then carried by teams of runners to the city that hosts the games.

MODERN GAMES

Fifteen hundred years after the last ancient Olympic, a French nobleman named Baron Pierre de Coubertin dreamed of reviving the games. At the same time, he did not want the new Olympics to be just a sports competition. He felt that the Olympics could be an event that also taught sportsmanship. In 1896, the first modern Olympic Games were held in Athens. Some of the events, like races, javelin throwing, the long jump, and wrestling are still Olympic events.

One modern event has its roots in ancient Greece. The marathon race is named for the distance run by the Greek soldier Pheidippides (fi–DIHP–uh–deez). In 490 B.C., Pheidippides ran from a battlefield near Marathon to Athens to report the news of the Greek victory over the Persians. He collapsed and died after his exhausting run. At 26 miles (42 kilometers), the marathon is the longest footrace in the Olympics.

In 2004, the Olympic Games returned to Athens for the summer games, which includes rowing among many other sports.

A Visit to D

Ruins of the sanctuary at Delphi

elphi

One of the ancient Greeks' most important and lasting creations was the stories they told about their gods and the holy places where they lived.

According to Greek **mythology,** Zeus, king of the gods, released two eagles, one from the east edge of the world and one from the west. Where the eagles met was the center of the Earth. The eagles met at Delphi, on the slopes of Mount Parnassus in central Greece. Zeus's son, Apollo, wanted his sanctuary to be at Delphi. To do this, Apollo first had to slay Python, an evil serpent that lived in the caves of Mount Parnassus.

Apollo's sanctuary at Delphi housed an **oracle.** An oracle (OR–uh–kuhl) is a place where the gods spoke to the ancient Greeks and gave them advice. The gods usually spoke through a priest, who was also called an oracle. Apollo's oracle at Delphi was a woman known as the Pythia (PITH–ee–uh), in honor of the god's victory over the serpent Python.

Apollo's Pythia in her trance while priests stand by to translate for the pilgrims

What Was In Those Vapors?

In the 1990s, scientists discovered two faults, or cracks, in the rock beneath the sanctuary at Delphi. They also found ethylene gas in spring water near the sanctuary.

They think that this gas may have seeped through the faults under the shrine and drugged Apollo's oracle. This may be why the Pythia muttered her strange words.

In ancient Greece, the place to go for advice from Apollo was Delphi. Before the ancient Greeks did anything important, they consulted his oracle. They asked questions about everything from planting crops to choosing a husband or wife.

Many **pilgrims,** people who journey to a holy place, came to Delphi. Visitors first went to the sacred spring there to take purifying baths. Then they climbed the Sacred Way, a winding path up the side of Mount Parnassus. At the top, was the Temple of Apollo.

Riddles from Apollo

After paying the priests of the sanctuary a set fee, someone seeking advice sacrificed an animal, usually a goat. Then, the priests submitted the visitor's question to the Pythia, who sat in the Temple's inner shrine on a three-legged stool called a tripod. The tripod was placed over a crack in the ground through which came vapors from deep within the Earth. These vapors sent the Pythia into a trance that enabled her to receive Apollo's word. In her trance state, the Pythia began to speak mysterious words. Other priests standing nearby translated her mutterings into lines of poetry for the pilgrim.

The advice from the oracle was not always clear, however. Often the statements were like riddles, and pilgrims had to guess what Apollo meant. One famous example of the oracle's vague advice is told in the story of King Croesus (KREES–uhs) of the country of Lydia. He asked the oracle whether he should go to war against the armies of Persia. The oracle replied that if he did so, he would destroy a great kingdom. Delighted with the answer, Croesus went to war and was beaten. He had failed to realize that the oracle's answer might mean that *his* kingdom was the one that would be destroyed.

The oracle at Delphi remained popular for centuries. With the rise of Christianity, however, people began to abandon the sanctuary at Delphi. In A.D. 390, the Roman emperor Theodosius, himself a Christian, ordered the Temple of Apollo at Delphi officially closed.

▶ *For more information about Greek mythology, see page 58.*

WHY IT MATTERS TODAY

Throughout history, people have held many places to be sacred or holy. These may be natural sites, such as caves and springs, that are linked to a people's beliefs. Or they may be towns or cities that are the locations of important religious shrines. From ancient times to the present, pilgrims have visited these places to worship, be blessed or cured, or seek help in troubled times.

THE
GREAT

Of all the Greek city-states, the two most powerful—and most completely different—were Athens and Sparta. Their rivalry would contribute to both the rise and fall of Greek civilization.

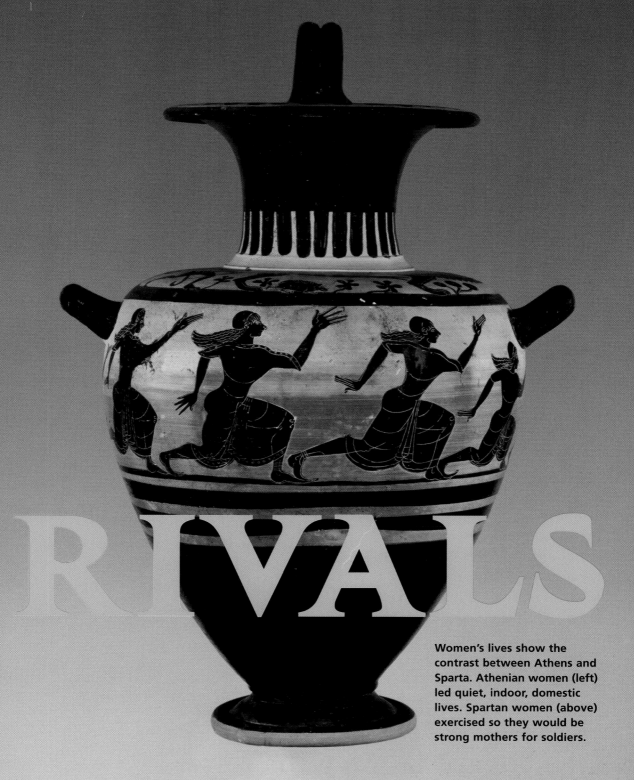

RIVALS

Women's lives show the contrast between Athens and Sparta. Athenian women (left) led quiet, indoor, domestic lives. Spartan women (above) exercised so they would be strong mothers for soldiers.

In this painting, one boy plays a lyre (left) while a teacher helps another boy learn to read (center and right).

Life in Athens

Athenians enjoyed freedom and creativity. They valued the arts and freedom of thought. Drama was particularly important in Athens. Athenians saw going to the theater as a civic responsibility, because their playwrights discussed important social and religious issues. Greek theaters were built into sloping hillsides and could hold up to 15,000 people. The stage was a flat surface at the bottom of the hill. Both comedies and tragedies were performed during the day as part of religious festivals. The actors were all men, and they wore costumes and masks.

Athenian boys were sent to school at age six. There they learned to read, write, and recite poetry. They also learned mathematics, music, and gymnastics. At age 18, they were eligible for military service, in which they spent two years as trainees. After military service they could become citizens, a great honor. Athenian girls were given no formal schooling and seldom left their homes, but many still learned to read and play musical instruments, such as the lyre, a kind of harp.

Like Sparta, Athens had an army, but it was called up only in response to specific outward dangers. Athenian armies were led by temporary generals, each elected to serve for a year. The people of Athens, like those of Sparta,

The goal of education in Sparta (above) was solely to produce soldiers (right).

also had a large number of slaves. Some served the households, while the rest worked on the farms or in various trades.

Life in Sparta

Spartans wanted order and strength. They were ruled by kings, and nearly every part of life was controlled by law. The men lived in barracks, visiting their families from time to time. At age seven, all healthy boys were taken to the men's barracks to live and be trained. There, they learned fighting skills and to be tough and obey rules. They learned to live on little food, and they were trained to spy and even to

steal if necessary. When they were 20 years old, they entered the army, where they served until they were 60.

Spartan girls got physical training too. They practiced running, wrestling, and throwing the discus and javelin. They received little other education, however. They were supposed to learn how to run a home and take care of a family when they grew up. Basically, they had one purpose in life—to become healthy mothers of healthy children. They were still freer than Athenian girls, however, in that they could take part in processions and certain feasts. A large group of people called **helots** (HEL–uhts) did much of the daily work in Sparta. Helots were conquered people who were treated as slaves. A special class of men ran businesses and trades.

Spartan leaders frowned on luxuries because they believed these made people soft and lazy. Spartans were not supposed to desire riches, and no Spartan was to have any more wealth than another Spartan. Their early lawgiver Lycurgus had wanted to keep them from hoarding wealth. So, he banned the use of gold and silver coinage. Spartan money was iron bars, which were heavy and not worth much. One Greek said a small room was needed to hold much of this iron money, and a pair of oxen was needed to move it.

Outsiders were not welcome in Sparta. Spartan leaders were afraid foreign ways might corrupt Spartan youth. The Spartans became skilled at providing for themselves. They made their own simple furniture and any other items they thought necessary for living. One typical Spartan design was a cup that made it less nasty for a soldier on the march to drink muddy water from a ditch.

The Two Cities

Athens was a crossroads of the ancient Mediterranean world, a busy trade center and an important seaport.

It made its own money, which was eventually used throughout the area. Athenian coins showed an owl, the symbol of their city's protector, the goddess Athena. The center of Athens was the **Acropolis,** a rocky hill. Athenians took pride in the richly decorated temples and other buildings that stood atop the Acropolis. In contrast, the Spartans scorned any outward show, and they built very little. Sparta did not trade with other city-states, in part because no other Greeks wanted the Spartans' iron money. The Spartans had little interest in art, drama, or literature.

The Acropolis of Athens and (right) one of the city's coins

From Allies to Enemies

Athens and Sparta fought as allies when the forces of the Persian Empire attacked Greece. The powerful combination of Athens's navy and Sparta's army helped Greece defeat these invaders. However, Athens then used its sea power to build an empire. Sparta feared its rival's new strength, and the two city-states became bitter enemies. Between 431 and 404 B.C., they fought a great war, called the Peloponnesian War, to see which of them would rule the Greek world. Sparta defeated Athens in the end, but there was no real winner. Both sides were worn out. They were too weak to resist the next invasion, this time from the region north of Greece known as Macedon or Macedonia.

▶ *For more information about Athens and Sparta, see pages 59–62.*

WHY IT MATTERS TODAY

In ancient Greece, rivalry between Athens and Sparta and the sharply differing ways of life in the two city-states brought a war that destroyed Greece. Throughout history, similar sets of circumstances have led to conflict and civil war.

The ruins of Sparta (left); Rusted remains of its iron money (bottom); Greek troops armed with spears marching into battle in a tight formation (below)

31

The Parthenon: Home for a *Goddess*

The Parthenon, the temple of the Greek goddess Athena on the Acropolis in Athens, is one of the most famous buildings in the world. It shows the Greek ideals of beauty and harmony that are an important part of what we call classical art.

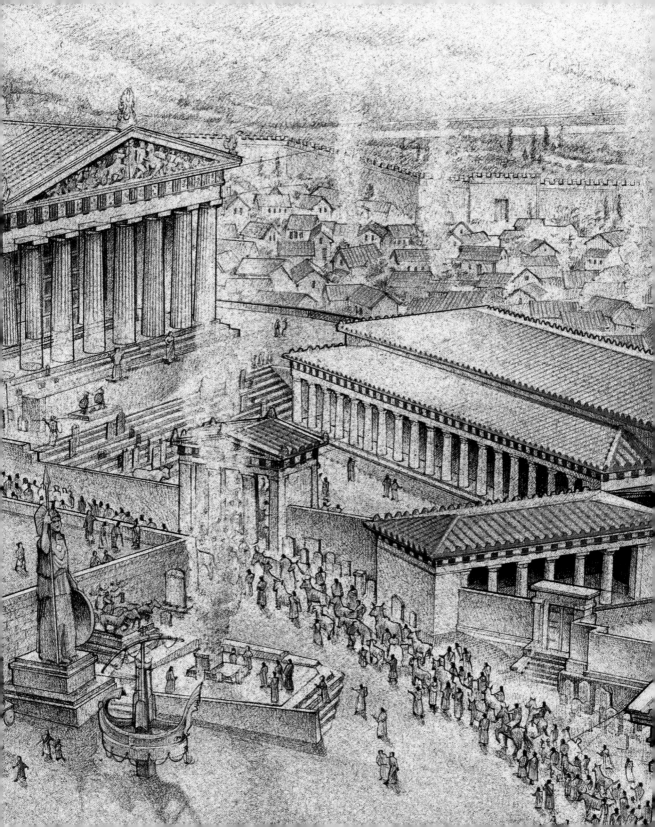

Balance and Harmony

In a Greek house, a young woman lived in a *parthenon* (maiden's room) before she married. To the Athenians, their city's goddess, Athena, had the beauty and grace of a young girl. Between 447 and 432 B.C., the Athenians built a temple for her. They wanted Athena's temple, which they called the **Parthenon** (PAHR–thuh–non), to show these qualities too. They succeeded. The Parthenon was one of the greatest achievements of the Golden Age.

The ancient Greeks valued harmony in their art. This meant that all the parts of a statue or a building should work together so that the whole looked balanced and in proportion. To give the Parthenon harmony, its builders kept the same ratio, or mathematical relationship, between the sizes and spacing of many parts of the temple. For example, this ratio exists between the Parthenon's length and width. The same ratio exists between the temple's width and the height of its columns.

For a Greek temple, the Parthenon is large, 230 feet (70 meters) long and 100 feet (30 meters) wide. Its builders used some tricks to keep the temple from looking heavy.

The Greeks knew that when we view a wide building from a distance, the lines of its base and roof often seem to sag slightly in the middle. The Parthenon's base and rooflines curve upward slightly, so they appear straight. Greek builders also knew that, from a distance, straight columns appear to curve inwards. They designed the Parthenon's columns with a slight outward bulge, so the sides look straight.

Athena

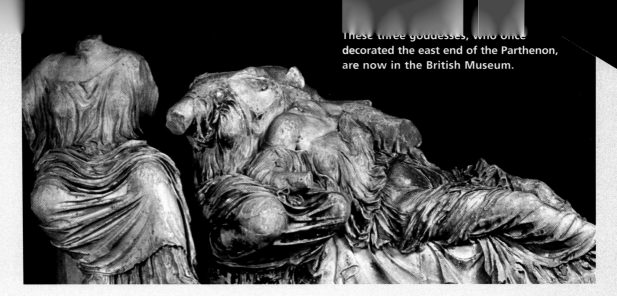

These three goddesses, who once decorated the east end of the Parthenon, are now in the British Museum.

Building the Parthenon

Athenians lived by three rules: "Honor the gods; help your friends; adorn your city." When the Athenian leader Pericles (pair–uh–KLEEZ) ordered the building of the Parthenon, he honored the goddess Athena. He gave work to his fellow citizens, who worked as carpenters, stonecutters, sculptors, ivory carvers, goldsmiths, and painters. And Pericles created something—as a later Greek writer noted—"for all time."

Pericles hired his friend, the sculptor Phidias (FIHD–ee–uhs), to supervise the building of the Parthenon. Under his direction, Athenian sculptors carved hundreds of figures to decorate Athena's temple. One was a continuous **frieze** (freez), or panel, 525 feet (160 meters) in length. This panel ran along the top of the Parthenon's side walls. It showed the procession held every four years to honor Athena.

In the early 1800s, a British diplomat, Lord Elgin, removed many of the sculptures from the Parthenon and took them to London. They are now in the British Museum. For many years, the Greek government has unsuccessfully tried to get back these sculptures, known as the "Parthenon Marbles."

▶ *For more information on the Golden Age of Athens, see pages 60–61.*

WHY IT MATTERS TODAY

The classical art of the ancient Greeks was a major influence on later artists. The influence of Greek architecture was very strong at the time of the American Revolution. Ever since, many American government buildings have been built in what is called a *neoclassical* style.

The Power of the PEOPLE

Athens was not ruled by a king, but by ordinary male citizens. With all its imperfections—women, slaves, and foreigners could not vote—Athenian democracy was one of the greatest legacies of ancient Greece.

Athenians later voted to exile fellow citizens by putting their names on broken bits of pottery (left).

Legendary Greek warriors cast votes by placing pebbles in a bowl (below).

The rich Athenian was scared! He squirmed as his fellow citizens dropped bits of broken pottery, called *ostraka,* into a container. It's true that he had been outspoken about the government, but did that make him a threat to the peace of Athens? If 6,000 voters scratched his name on their ostrakon, he would have to leave Athens for ten years! **Ostracism** (OS–truh–siz–uhm), or exile, was the way that Athenians kept any one person from gaining too much power. After all, Athens was where the people ruled themselves, instead of being ruled by a king.

It had not always been this way. Before democracy was established in Athens, an **aristocracy** (ahr–ih–STOK–ruh–see), or upper class, held most of the power. Instead of using their power for the good of all the people, the aristocrats were selfish. They forced small farmers to work the land for next to nothing. Deeply in debt, the farmers were little more than slaves.

The aristocrats feared a revolt. They could lose everything they owned. So, they looked for a leader who could find answers to the problems of Athens.

Athenians discussed issues of the day in the center of their city.

They found one in a wise, inspiring statesman named Solon. The first thing Solon did was cancel all debts. Then, he reduced the power of the aristocrats. He divided the people into four groups by income, making wealth, not family or social position, the basis for citizenship. Solon opened the way for any male citizen to hold public office. All men had to do was work hard and increase their wealth.

When Athenians wanted to exercise their right to vote, they went to the Assembly. Meetings of the Assembly were held every ten days on a hillside east of the Acropolis. Up to 6,000 people would attend to listen to political speeches and vote for leaders and laws. Votes were mostly taken with a show of hands.

The Assembly was noisy with political speeches and gossip. Like the U.S. Congress, it met regularly to make recommendations or give advice. The Assembly decided everything in Athens, from the price of olives to taxes and declarations of war. Each man had one vote. It was called "the rule of many."

An important feature of Athenian democracy was the Council. The Council was a smaller, more elite group than the Assembly. Only the Council could propose laws. Only the Assembly could vote on them. In this way, the Council and Assembly kept a balance of political power in Athens.

Only the best arguments given at the Assembly would convince people to vote one way or another. Learning how to use persuasive language was highly valued in Athens. Public speaking was the most important subject taught in Athenian schools.

Limits to Freedom

Democracy in Athens was limited. Only citizens could vote in the Assembly, and only free males over 18 years of age were citizens. Athenian women could not participate in government and were allowed little chance to join in any public life. Neither slaves—who were one-third of the population of Athens—nor foreigners could be citizens.

Exercising freedom of speech in Athens could sometimes be dangerous. The great Athenian thinker, Socrates (SOK–ruh–teez), urged his students to question everything, including Athenian traditions and beliefs about the gods. He said his role was to be a kind of "gadfly" whose stinging would help keep Athens moving in the right direction.

However, some Athenians accused Socrates of corrupting the youth of Athens and threatening their way of life. He was found guilty and sentenced to death by drinking poison. His friends urged him to flee Athens, but Socrates refused to abandon his city, even though it had condemned him to death. He drank the poison, dying in obedience to Athenian law.

▶ *For more information about Greek government and about Socrates, see pages 58–59 and pages 60–61.*

WHY IT MATTERS TODAY

Our word *politics* comes from *polis* (POH–lihs), the Greek word for city-state. Many of our political ideas, including democracy itself, come from ancient Greece.

Socrates

Judges used bronze discs to show their judgments. A hollow handle meant guilty.

DEMOCRACY

Sonia Gandhi, head of one of India's largest political parties, in a recent election campaign

The ancient Greek government has inspired similar democracies throughout the world. Americans elect representatives to the Congress, the part of the U.S. government that makes the laws. As in Athens, the American lawmakers are divided into a large group, the House of Representatives, and a smaller one, the Senate. Like the Assembly and Council of Athens, the two divisions of the U.S. Congress have different responsibilities and help check each other's power.

As in Athens, members of Congress give speeches that try to persuade other representatives to support an issue.

Unlike in Athens, women are allowed to be representatives, and nobody is required to be wealthy to run for an office.

In Athens, whoever wanted to vote on an issue would go to the Assembly. In Brazil's modern democracy, however, people are required to vote. Almost every citizen between the ages of 18 and 70 must, at the very least, show up to a voting location on election day.

The largest democracy in the world today is neither European nor American—it's Asian. India, with a population of more than one billion people, elects up to 795 people to its legislature!

PROBLEM
SOLVERS

HIPPOCRATES

ARCHIMEDES

The ancient Greeks created a new way of thinking based on the use of reason, or thinking based on reliable evidence. They used this new way of thinking to examine many aspects of life, from the movement of the planets to the treatment of diseases.

Imagine going to the doctor and being told that the reason you are sick is that you have made the gods angry. Imagine believing that the world is flat and that the sky is held above the Earth by a giant pillar or column. These were common beliefs in the ancient world. Most ancient peoples used religion and myths to explain what happened around them.

The Greeks, however, began to look at things differently. They embraced a new way of thinking that emphasized **logic,** reasoning, mathematics, and careful observation. The result was an explosion in scientific knowledge. Two of the greatest Greek scientists were a doctor named Hippocrates (hih–POK–ruh–teez) and an inventor and mathematician named Archimedes (ahr–kuh–MEE–deez).

The Father of Medicine

Hippocrates, born about 460 B.C., was the leader of a medical school on the Greek island of Kos. He traveled throughout Greece and the Middle East, teaching and practicing medicine. According to legend, wherever he went he cured diseases and ridded grateful cities of **plagues.**

When Hippocrates began teaching, medical treatment depended heavily on praying, driving out demons, and giving gifts to the gods to get back in their good favor. Hippocrates challenged this view. He believed that illness had a logical, physical explanation. He taught his medical students to interview patients, observe the course of diseases and treatments, and record results. He is often called "the Father of Medicine."

Hippocrates and his followers were the first to accurately describe the symptoms of many diseases. They supported the idea that thoughts and feelings originate in the brain, rather than in the heart, as most people then believed. They recognized that there was a link between illness and the environment. The books they wrote about surgery, anatomy, and how to diagnose and treat diseases formed the greatest medical library of the time.

Hippocrates believed that doctors should practice the highest ethics. He created a code of conduct called the Hippocratic Oath. Today, when doctors receive their medical degrees, many swear a modern version of the Hippocratic Oath.

Mathematician and Inventor

Archimedes was born about 287 B.C. in the city of Syracuse on the island of Sicily. He solved mathematical problems that no one had solved before. He developed new ideas about the ways that objects move and exert force on one another. He enjoyed putting his theories to practical use. He sometimes became so involved in his work that he forgot to eat. He had no paper to draw on, so he used everything from the dust on the ground to ashes from a cold fire to draw his geometric figures.

One day when he was getting into the bath, Archimedes noticed that as each part of his body entered the bath, the water overflowed a little more. According to legend, he used this observation to help the king of Syracuse learn whether a new crown, which was supposed to be made of pure gold, was in fact partly silver.

Archimedes sank a mass of silver, known to weigh the same as the crown, into a container filled to the top with water. He measured the amount of water that overflowed. Then, he refilled the container to the brim. He sank a mass of gold, known to weigh the same as the crown, into the container. He noticed that less water overflowed. The lumps of gold and silver weighed the same, but the silver lump was bigger because silver is lighter than gold.

A Greek doctor attends to a wound (left); Archimedes works on a geometry problem as a Roman soldier prepares to kill him (right).

He then refilled the container and sank the crown into it. More water overflowed than it did for the mass of gold. The king had been cheated.

When Roman ships attacked Syracuse, Archimedes came to the city's defense. He built catapults, machines that hurled boulders at the Roman fleet. He created hooks, or claws, attached to chains that lifted ships out of the water by means of a lever. The ships were then dropped back into the water and either overturned or sank. He is believed to have set ships on fire by using specially shaped mirrors to focus sunlight on their sails.

The Romans conquered Syracuse in spite of Archimedes's inventions. Legend has it that Archimedes was so absorbed in a geometry problem that he did not notice the city had been taken.

He was drawing circles when a Roman soldier ordered him to move. Archimedes refused to leave until he had worked out his problem. The soldier killed him on the spot. Archimedes last words were, "Don't disturb my circles."

▶ *For more information about Greek thought, see pages 60–61.*

▶ *For more information about Greek thought, see pages 60–61.*

WHY IT MATTERS TODAY

The desire to understand the world around them led the Greeks to ask many questions. Their answers to these questions were often wrong. But the Greek approach, using observation and reason, was the basis for later science, mathematics, and medicine.

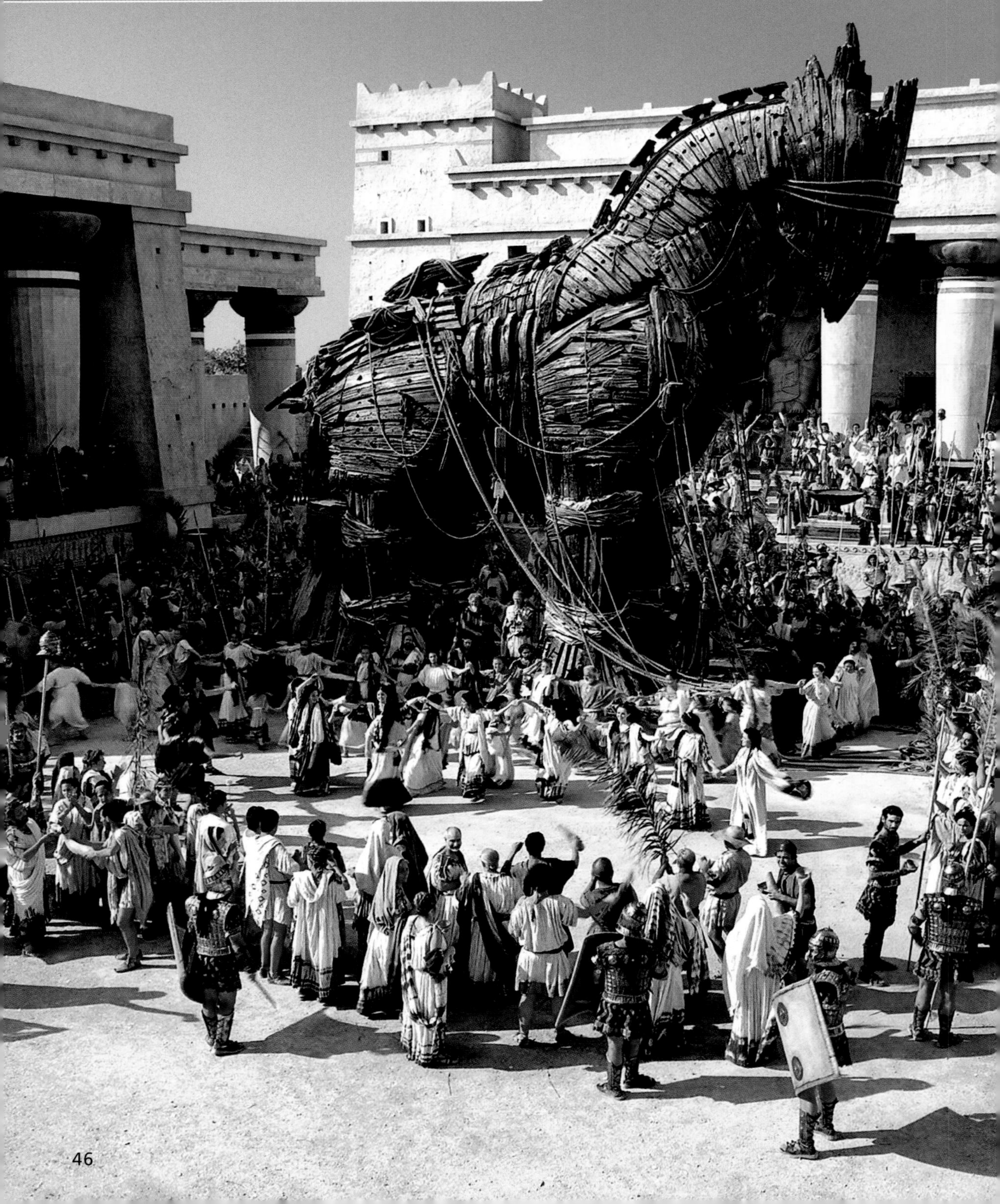

IN SEARCH OF TROY

The history of ancient Greece lives on in its stories. One of the most important legacies of the ancient Greeks was the tales they told of their gods and heroes. Of all these stories, none was more famous than the legend of the Trojan War.

A modern artist's conception of the Trojan Horse (left)

An ancient Greek vase painting of Helen of Troy and the Trojan king, Priam (above)

Homer probably composed the *Iliad* sometime between 725 and 675 B.C.

To the ancient Greeks, the **Trojan War** was the greatest event in their history. Their ancestors, the Mycenaeans (mi–suh–NEE–uhns), fought and won a long war against a city called Troy. The Greeks were as certain that this had happened as we are that the colonists fought the British in the American Revolution.

The ancient Greeks knew about the Trojan War because their most important poet, Homer, had told the story in his long poem, the *Iliad*. (The title refers to Ilium, another name for Troy.) Here's the story. A Trojan prince steals a beautiful Greek woman named Helen from her husband, a Greek king. To get Helen back, the Greeks attack Troy.

After ten years of war, the Greeks are no closer to breaking through Troy's great walls than they were at the start. Then, they come up with a clever idea to get into the city. They build a huge wooden horse and hide Greek soldiers in its belly. Pretending to depart Troy, they leave the horse outside the gates of the city. The Trojans, thinking the horse is a gift, take the horse inside the city walls. That night, the Greek warriors creep out and open the gates for the rest of their army. They burn Troy, kill its men, and take its women as slaves. All during the war, the Greek gods watch the fighting from Mount Olympus. Some aid the Greeks, and others help the Trojans.

Was It True?

Certainly the story of the Trojan War is exciting. It is filled with heroes and battles and magic, like *The Lord of the Rings*. But is it true? Is it really history as the ancient Greeks had believed? As time went by, people grew more and more certain that the Trojan War was mostly legend. Maybe there was some truth in the old tale, but who knew how much?

Then, about 130 years ago, a man named Heinrich Schliemann (SHLEE–muhn) made a discovery that changed the way people saw Troy.

Schliemann had loved Homer's story about Troy since he had read it as a child in a book his father had given him. Schliemann believed Troy had been a real place, and he decided to prove it.

Schliemann became a self-made millionaire, so he had the time and money to pursue his dream. He traveled around the world, learning about ancient history and archaeology. By chance, Schliemann met an Englishman, Frank Calvert, who was also interested in finding Troy. Calvert had been digging in northwest Turkey. He thought the ancient city was buried under a high mound called Hisarlik (HIH–sahr–lihk), a Turkish word meaning "fortress." Calvert was running out of money, so he shared his theory with his wealthy new friend. Schliemann agreed to pay the costs and direct the digging. In 1871, serious excavation work began at Hisarlik.

Hisarlik was more than 100 feet (30 meters) high. Schliemann and his workers began by digging a large trench through it. Immediately, Schliemann saw clearly marked layers of remains. Each layer marked where a new city was built on the ruins of an earlier one. He identified nine layers.

A reconstruction of Troy based on the excavations at Hisarlik

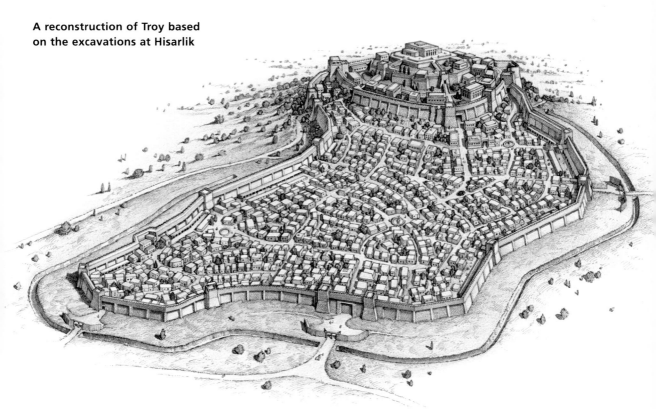

Schliemann believed he would find the legendary city of Troy in the lowest layers. Between 1871 and 1873, his men dug through the upper ones. In May 1873, in the second layer from the bottom, Schliemann finally found what he thought was the evidence he needed—treasure. He found cups of gold, silver, and bronze, vases, copper spearheads, and thousands of pieces of gold jewelry. Schliemann believed he had found the treasure of Priam, the king of Troy in the *Iliad*.

Schliemann's discovery caused a sensation. His reports from Hisarlik were published and were wildly popular. To his delight, he became famous.

Schliemann had no proof for his claim that Hisarlik was the site of Troy. Some experts, including Calvert, challenged many of his statements about his discoveries. They were right. Later archaeological research has shown that the level of "Priam's Treasure" is far too early to be Homer's Troy.

These ruined walls at Hisarlik are from the level whose date matches that of Homer's Troy.

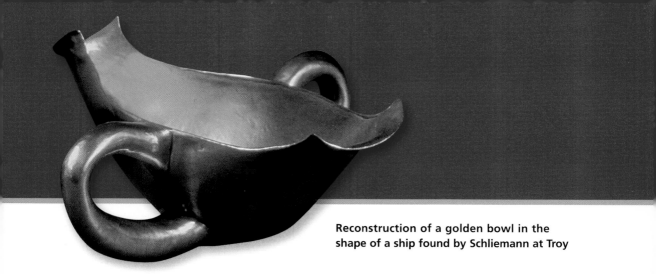

Reconstruction of a golden bowl in the shape of a ship found by Schliemann at Troy

Schliemann's fame also hid other problems. He had agreed that half of what he found would be given to a Turkish museum. Instead, Schliemann smuggled all the valuable objects out of the country. Most of them he gave to museums in Europe. He had also agreed that he would not damage the ruins. But Schliemann's crude digging methods destroyed large portions of the site. He also kept poor records.

Although Schliemann was not a careful researcher, he was very important in the history of archaeology. He excavated a number of important ancient Greek sites. His discoveries excited the general public and made many people interested in archaeology.

Most important, it now seems that Schliemann was basically right. Troy was in fact a real city where a war like the one in the *Iliad* could have taken place. Dr. Manfred Korfmann is a German archaeologist who has been directing research at Troy since 1988. He believes that the fortifications found there indicate that the city of Troy was large and rich enough to be worth fighting over. Even though Korfmann's finds at the site are different from Homer's description of Troy in points of detail, he feels the ancient story has a basis in fact.

▶ *For more information about the Trojan War, see pages 57–58.*

WHY IT MATTERS TODAY

The Greek legend of the Trojan War is one of the most influential tales ever told. To take just one example, the ancient Romans linked their own origins to Troy by making the founders of their city the descendants of a Trojan prince. From Homer's tales to the most recent Hollywood movie version, the tale of Troy has entertained and inspired people for more than 2,500 years.

One of the most famous legends of Alexander describes how he tamed a fierce horse named Bucephalus that he rode throughout his later campaigns.

Alexander
THE GREAT

Alexander and his warhorse Bucephalus in battle

WORLD CLASS HERO

Alexander the Great was one of the most skillful and daring soldiers of all time. Through his many conquests, he also spread Greek culture throughout much of the ancient world.

Alexander was born in Macedon, a region north of Greece. Although he began his conquests by defeating the Greeks, Alexander was himself Greek in culture. His teacher had been the great Greek thinker Aristotle. On his campaigns, Alexander always kept a copy of Homer's *Iliad* with him. As a conqueror, he championed Greek ways, founding many cities on the Greek model throughout his empire. Alexander of Macedon died of a fever at the age of 33. His short career as a soldier was over, but the legends about Alexander the Great had just begun to grow. Like Achilles, the greatest hero in the *Iliad*, Alexander lives on as the ideal warrior.

Greek Tales

Within a hundred years after Alexander's death, an unknown Greek writer collected many legends about him. One famous story says that Alexander wanted to see the wonders of the deep. He ordered his craftsmen to make a big glass jar and attach a long chain to it. Alexander got into the jar, and ordered his men to lower him to the seafloor. As Alexander went deeper and deeper, all kinds of strange fish swam around him. Finally, a huge fish seized the jar in its mouth and swam off. It spit Alexander onto a beach about a mile away, leaving him gasping and terrified.

Alexander the Great exploring the sea in a glass diving bell

Arabic Legends

The Arabs told many stories about Alexander. In a famous Arabic legend, he led a group of his men on a search for the Fountain of Life. Its water would make a person live forever. One day, Alexander's cook went off from the rest to look for some water to prepare dried fish for a meal. He found a pool and began to wash the fish. As soon as the fish touched the water, they came to life and swam off. The cook then drank from the pool, which made him immortal, but also turned his skin green. Of course, Alexander wanted to rediscover the pool, but now it could not be found. He became angry at his cook and tried to kill him in different ways, but the cook was now immortal.

The Middle Ages

In the Middle Ages, people saw Alexander as a noble knight, like one of those at King Arthur's court. One tale from that time says that Porus, a king of India, sent a letter to Alexander, challenging him to single combat. Whoever won would rule Porus's kingdom. Porus was nearly twice as tall as Alexander, so he expected an easy victory. Both kings armed themselves, mounted their horses, leveled their spears at one another, and charged. At the impact, their spears splintered, but neither king was unhorsed. Porus pulled out his sword and struck Alexander on his helmet. Alexander struck back, and his blow was so fierce that it knocked Porus out of his saddle and threw him to the ground, senseless. Alexander had his men take off Porus's helmet to give the king air. Later, Porus gave his kingdom to Alexander, but Alexander gave it back, and the two kings became friends.

▶ *For more information about Alexander the Great, see page 62.*

WHY IT MATTERS TODAY

Legends about Alexander the Great from around the world reflect his cultural legacy. By conquering Greece, Alexander destroyed the independence of the Greek city-states. But the long-term effect of his conquests was the spread of Greek culture throughout his vast empire from Egypt to India. In turn, Greek culture blended with Egyptian, Persian, and other ancient cultures into a new civilization.

Greek Civilization

This Overview provides a brief summary of the most important people, places, and events of ancient Greece. Its purpose is to help you better understand the historical background of the articles in this book.

The Geography of Greece

Greece is a peninsula at the southeastern tip of Europe. Hundreds of islands, also part of Greece, surround the peninsula. Much of Greece is mountainous. Mount Olympus, in myth the home of the Greek gods, rises to more than 9,000 feet (2,700 meters). Because of the rocky soil, which makes farming difficult, early Greeks settled along the coasts where they raised olives, grapes, and other crops suited to the mild climate.

Three seas border Greece—the Mediterranean, the Aegean, and the Ionian. The early Greeks became excellent shipbuilders, navigators, and sailors. Land travel in ancient times was almost impossible because of the many rugged mountains, so the Greeks carried on their trade with Asian and African cities by sea.

The Minoans

Around 2000 B.C., a seafaring people on the large island of Crete (kreet) in the eastern Mediterranean Sea created a prosperous society based on trade. They are known today as the Minoans (mih–NOH–uhns), from the name of a legendary Cretan king named Minos. The Minoans had a great influence on Greek civilization.

Major Events

1300 B.C.		900 B.C.	

1250 B.C.
Traditional date of Trojan War

776 B.C.
First Olympic Games

725 B.C.
Iliad composed

The Minoans owed their wealth in part to the rich natural resources of Crete, which included wheat, wine, olive oil, and wool. Their other major assets were timber and the know-how to build seaworthy ships. Their ships helped the Minoans dominate trade in the eastern Mediterranean.

Trade stimulated Minoan crafts, which included finely decorated pottery, colorful woolens, and gold and silver drinking vessels and daggers. There were several kingdoms on Crete, and their rulers used wealth gained through trade to build richly decorated palaces connected with paved roads.

Temple to Poseidon, god of the sea

The Mycenaeans

Around 1450 B.C., a warrior people from mainland Greece overran Crete. They are known today as the Mycenaeans. Their ancestors had migrated into Greece from

the north and spoke an early form of the Greek language. The Mycenaeans were organized into many small kingdoms, each of which had its own hilltop fortress commanding the surrounding farmlands. The most impressive of these was Mycenae, from which their culture takes its name. Protected by a high, thick stone wall, Mycenae was a powerful fortress.

Mycenaean gold mask

490 B.C.
Battle of Marathon

432 B.C.
Parthenon completed

323 B.C.
Death of
Alexander the Great

650 B.C.

300 B.C.

c. 480 B.C.
Beginning of Golden
Age of Athens

404 B.C.
Sparta defeats
Athens

Life in Ancient Greece

According to legend, Mycenaeans fought and won a war with Troy, a city in what is now Turkey. Historians once believed that the story of this war caused by a beautiful woman named Helen was just a legend, but around 1870 a German archaeologist discovered layers of nine cities, each built on top of the previous one. Did he find Troy? Today, historians believe that he did and that a Trojan War actually took place, though no one really knows what caused the war.

The Dorians

Around 1200 B.C., soon after the Trojan War, the Mycenaean civilization declined and another gradually took its place among the ruined cities. A people called the Dorians migrated from the north into Greece. They enslaved many Greeks, and Greek civilization declined. In fact, Greek writing disappeared. Not until some time in the 700s B.C. did the Greeks develop their alphabet. Many historians think that the words of the poet Homer were first written down about this time.

The Gods of Olympus

One of ancient Greece's gifts to the world was its mythology, the famous stories of its gods. The following are the names, functions, and family relationships of the most important Greek gods.

Zeus (zoos) god of the sky; king of the gods

Poseidon (puh–SI–don) god of the sea; brother of Zeus

Hades (HAY–deez) ruler of the dead; brother of Zeus

Hera (HAIR–uh) queen of the gods; wife of Zeus

Demeter (dih–MEE–ter) goddess of the harvest; sister of Zeus

Hephaestus (hih–FES–tuhs) god of fire and metalwork; son of Hera

Ares (AIR–eez) god of war; son of Zeus

Aphrodite (af–roh–DI–tee) goddess of love and beauty; daughter of Zeus

Hermes (HER–meez) messenger of the gods; son of Zeus

Athena (uh–THEE–nuh) goddess of wisdom; daughter of Zeus

Apollo (uh–POL–oh) god of inspiration and art; son of Zeus

Artemis (AHR–tuh–mis) goddess of the hunt and the moon; daughter of Zeus

Dionysus (DI–oh–NI–sus) god of wine; son of Zeus

The Rise of City-States

Early Greek communities were separated from each other by geography. So, they became politically independent. These communities formed city-states. A city-state, called a *polis,* consisted of an independent city and the country around it, including small villages. Greek city-states were governed in a number of ways over the years. At first, kings or monarchs ruled in a monarchy. Then, a wealthy group of landowners ruled in an aristocracy. Discontented residents revolted against this rule, however, and powerful

Greek vote-casting disk

The Greek gods (left to right) Poseidon, Apollo, and Artemis

leaders, called *tyrants,* emerged. Later, wealthy merchants gained power and ruled in an oligarchy, which means "rule by a few." Eventually, some city-states, such as Athens, were ruled by citizens in a democracy. Two rival city-states, Athens and Sparta, were vastly different in their style of life and in their government.

Athens

In an early Greek democracy, such as the one in Athens, only male citizens could vote. Women, slaves, and foreigners could not.

In Athens, life centered about the marketplace, or *agora,* the theater, and temples. In the marketplace, people sold what they had grown or made. Playgoers attended comedies or tragedies in a large outdoor theater built into the side of a hill. The center of Athens was a rocky hill called the Acropolis. Several temples stood on the Acropolis, but the most important of these was the Parthenon. Here, worshipers offered animal sacrifices to Athena, goddess of war, wisdom, and art.

Sparta

Life in the city-state of Sparta could not have been more different from life in Athens. Spartan government was complicated. Two kings trained the Spartan army. All adult males made up an Assembly. In addition, a council of elders proposed laws. Finally, five people called *ephors* held most of the power. Three classes of people lived in Sparta: the ruling class who owned the land; free men who were not citizens but who were farmers and artisans; people called *helots* who worked as servants. Helots were treated as slaves; they were not free.

The Spartan way of life was intended to prepare citizens for war. At the age of seven, boys left home and started military training. They marched shoeless, ate small meals, and slept on hard benches. Spartan girls were trained as athletes. Soldiers lived in barracks, even when they were married, and served until they were 60 years of age.

The Persian Wars

The Persian Wars were fought between Greece and the Persian Empire. This conflict began when the Persians took control of Greek city-states along the coast of Asia Minor (modern Turkey) in 546 B.C. These city-states, supported by Athens, finally rebelled in 499 B.C. Persia invaded mainland Greece to punish Athens. But in 490 B.C., the Athenians won a great victory over the Persians at Marathon, a plain near Athens.

The Golden Age

After this defeat, the Persians were determined to conquer all of Greece. They began to build a great army and navy. The Athenians also began to build a great navy. When the two enemies met again in a sea battle at Salamis, the Athenians won again. The Spartans then defeated the Persians on land in a third battle.

The Greeks were still wary of the Persians, however, and 140 Greek city-states formed the Delian League to defend the country and to try to free those city-states still under Persian rule. Because Delian League members paid taxes to Athens, it soon became the richest and most important city-state in Greece.

The Golden Age of Athens

The Golden Age of Athens lasted from about 480 to 430 B.C. This period of political power and cultural achievement is closely linked to the career of a wise Athenian leader named Pericles, who lived from about 495 to 429 B.C. He led Athens to a stronger democracy. Under Pericles, government positions were paid, and more citizens could serve than before. As Pericles himself said, "No one is kept in political obscurity because of poverty." However, only male citizens could serve in the government.

Greek Thinkers

A group of teachers and thinkers called Sophists were well known for their ideas about right and wrong. Boys were sent to learn from them so that they could become good citizens. A philosopher called Socrates was opposed to the Sophists, however. He tried, through questioning, to lead people to discover

Athena mourning for the men of Athens killed in battle

Sculptures support the porch of the Erechtheum, a building on the Acropolis at Athens.

great truths about life for themselves. He was considered dangerous, however. He was charged with corrupting the young and introducing new gods. As a result, Socrates was sentenced to death.

Socrates left no writings, but his pupil, Plato, did. In "The Apology," he presented the speech Socrates delivered at his trial. Plato wrote that Socrates said that he had done nothing more than persuade both young and old to care for their soul rather than for their body or wealth.

Greek Arts and Architecture

It was during the Golden Age that architects and sculptors created their finest work. Begun in 447 B.C., the Parthenon originally held a gigantic gold and ivory statue of the goddess Athena. Pericles was responsible for planning work on the Parthenon. When Athenians objected to the expense, he said, "We must devote ourselves to acquiring things that will be the source of everlasting fame." We know of his fame 2,500 years later.

Greek sculptors were superb at fashioning life-size human figures from bronze and marble. During the Golden Age, the faces of the figures often showed more expression than earlier works had, making them seem like images of real people.

The Greeks were enthusiastic playgoers. Greek drama grew out of religious ceremonies to celebrate various events. Tragedies written during the Golden Age dealt with themes involving right and wrong behavior, the fate of humans who suffer misfortune, and human interactions with the gods. Comedies were more concerned with interactions among humans.

The Peloponnesian War

Unfortunately, the Golden Age of Athens did not last. Sparta became increasingly jealous and even frightened of Athens's power and influence. Sparta, not a member of the Delian League, declared war against Athens in 431 B.C. The Spartans wanted to fight a land war and began to burn crops in an effort to starve the Athenians.

The Athenians had a superior navy, however, and Pericles thought that they could win the war at sea. After ten years of fighting, Sparta and Athens finally signed a truce, but scattered fighting continued. In 415 B.C., a member of the Athenian Assembly convinced the Athenians to force city-states on the island of Sicily to become part of the Athenian Empire. The Athenian army was captured, however, and much of the navy was defeated. Sparta then attacked Athens, as did the Persians. In 404 B.C., the Athenians surrendered to the Spartans. The Golden Age of Athens was ended.

Alexander the Great

In the middle of the 4th century B.C., several tribes in Macedon in the north of Greece united under a ruler named Philip. He was made king in 359 B.C. His ambitious son Alexander became king after Philip's death. Alexander first united all the Greeks and invaded Persia. He conquered a huge empire, from Macedon and Egypt in the west to the border of India in the east. He died in 323 B.C. at the age of 33. Known as Alexander the Great, his conquests spread Greek civilization throughout the Middle East. Greece itself declined, however, and was conquered by the Romans in 146 B.C.

The Greek Legacy

Greek ideas spread far beyond the borders of Greece. Greek mythology has provided a rich source of subjects for writers and artists. Greek drama, art, and architecture are known throughout the world. Democracy and science began with the Greeks. Most important, the Greeks introduced the idea that the individual person has value.

Alexander the Great and Bucephalus

GLOSSARY

Acropolis a hill at the center of Athens

archaeologist a scientist who studies the remains of peoples and cultures of the past

aristocracy an upper class

city-state a state made up of a city and its surrounding territory

colony a region controlled by another country

democracy government by the people

frieze a carved panel around a room or building

helot in Sparta, a conquered person who did much of the ordinary work and was treated as a slave

hoplite a Greek foot soldier who wore heavy armor

logic method of reasoning

mythology stories that deal with gods, goddesses, and heroes and that explain some part of the natural world, such as the seasons

Olympic Games the athletic contests held at Olympia every four years beginning in 776 B.C.

oracle a shrine where a priest tells the future; also, the priest

ostracism exile or banishment of a person considered a threat to the state

pankration an Olympic event that combined wrestling and boxing

Parthenon the temple on the Acropolis built to honor the goddess Athena

pentathlon an Olympic competition consisting of five separate events: a discus throw, a long jump, a javelin throw, a footrace, and a wrestling match

pilgrim a person who journeys to a holy place

plague a disease that spreads rapidly and usually causes death

sanctuary a sacred shrine

Trojan War the ten-year-long conflict that the ancient Greeks believed their ancestors had fought with the city of Troy about 1250 B.C.

INDEX